The Fruits
— of the —
Holy Spirit

Blessings!

Dr. Paul R. Kitley

The Fruits of the Holy Spirit

PAUL L. KITLEY

Providence House Publishers
WWW.PROVIDENCEHOUSE.COM
FRANKLIN, TENNESSEE

Printed in the United States of America

11   10   09   08   07   1   2   3   4   5

Library of Congress Control Number: 2007932918

ISBN: 978-1-57736-400-9

Cover illustration by LeAnna Massingille
Cover and page design by LeAnna Massingille

Scripture quotations are taken from HOLY BIBLE,
NEW INTERNATIONAL VERSION®. Copyright © 1973, 1978, 1984 by
International Bible Society. Used by permission of Zondervan Publishing House.

PROVIDENCE HOUSE PUBLISHERS
238 Seaboard Lane • Franklin, Tennessee 37067
www.providencehouse.com
800-321-5692

This book is dedicated to the memory of my wife,
Angela Justine Kitley,
and to our three grown children and their families.

Contents

Preface

As an ordained minister of some fifty-eight years, I believe more strongly than ever the worth of spirituality being the key factor affecting the totality of our existence. We human beings have a body, mind, and soul. Our biological situation is very important to our existence and deserves our attention in matters of proper nutrition. Awareness of our genetic backgrounds and understanding of the role disease plays in the role of our biological functions is necessary; our bodies deserve good doctoring, so to speak, to keep them functioning well.

We know much about the functioning of the brain and the many factors involved in what we may call healthy mental attitudes, positive thinking, and the part neurotransmitters play in keeping mental functioning at its best.

Spirituality deals with the soul. To be alive as human beings demands that we do not isolate the one component from the other, as if each can be dealt with separately. In other words, to be fully human involves the processes of how each part is inseparably tied in with the other—our body, mind, and soul are inseparably linked together and each affect the other.

Scientific research has shown that a healthy immune system enables the biological processes to impact a healthy attitude and a positive outlook on life. It has also been shown that the development of a positive outlook on life can, in turn, affect the immune system. For instance, constant stress can shut down the immune system and render one more vulnerable to viruses, bacteria, fungi, and destructive parasites.

Attention given to our spiritual outlook on life contributes greatly to our way of thinking, which, in turn, affects biological functions. The soul plays an important role in our total well being; our spirituality is what makes us fully human.

Spirituality involves:

- *the search for meaning in life*
- *values by which we live*
- *an understanding of mortality*
- *a concept of how the universe is organized and guided*
- *beliefs regarding the dilemma of suffering*
- *beliefs regarding the nature of transcendence*
- *beliefs regarding our existence beyond death*
- *beliefs regarding good and evil*
- *meaningful interactions with other human beings*
- *our relationship with the earth on which God placed us*

Based on my understanding of the Good News of God's Son, our Savior, Jesus Christ, and how it has fit into my professional experience as a counselor/therapist, I have developed five convictions. These will be elaborated on throughout this book.

1. I believe God loves us unconditionally. Such a concept may be difficult for some to believe since most relationships have a somewhat contractual character; it is hard to love someone who is unlovable. However, the essential picture of God is that He created us in His likeness.

   God does not enjoy punishing as a consequence for our sinful nature. However, due to our unwillingness to trust Him and accept His unconditional love, we punish ourselves, shutting the door on His unconditional love for our spiritual growth.

2. Just as we grow physically and mentally, we also can grow spiritually. In a sense, God became human in His son, Jesus, who is our best picture of God's purposes for us and His creation. He died for us through the crucifixion and, in Christ's resurrection, we have the one sure conviction of the power of growing in God's grace.

3. Spiritual growth occurs by practicing the presence of God in our lives through the Holy Spirit He has given us. By practicing healthy spiritual exercises we place ourselves in a context for the Holy Spirit to work within us, and the fruits of the Spirit (as Paul lists in Galatians) grow.

   Spiritual growth is how the Holy Spirit pervades our very being to create within us the continuous new creation in Christlikeness.

4. Sin is a disease of the soul, just as we have diseases of the body and mind. Perhaps at its core is pride—our unwillingness to trust completely in God's care for us because we must be completely in control.

5. We should think of God's commandments as God's spiritual nutrition laws. By participating in the work of the Holy Spirit in our lives, we can prepare ourselves to enjoy all the blessings God has for us in this life and the next to come. By choosing not to grow in God's likeness, we self-destruct. We condemn ourselves.

At the end of each chapter, I suggest a spiritual exercise for you to do called "Cultivating Spiritual Fruit." May God richly bless you and may the following provide some "helps" in your spiritual journey!

In Gratitude

Reflecting back over seventy-seven years, I am grateful for the many people who have impacted my life for the good. I had a very religious mother who saw to it that we were in Sunday school and church most every Sunday and a father who worked hard and was as honest as the day is long. I was reared on a farm a few miles east of Indianapolis and was the fifth in a family of seven boys. We learned to appreciate the value of work as well as the importance of sharing, and have been relatively close across the years.

My wife of fifty-seven-and-a-half years taught me much about compassion and reaching out to others, as did several teachers and college and seminary professors too numerous to mention. I am grateful to have served in supportive churches. In my later years, I have also been blessed to maintain helpful collegial relationships in my work as a counselor and chaplain for a hospital.

The content of this book reflects also the areas of my own personal and professional life in which I hope I have grown spiritually as a human being; I hope to continue to grow closer in my relationship to God and to share with others the gifts He has given me.

I thank my children for the years we have shared, especially my daughter, Angela Lynne Johnson, who lives near me and who has shared many helpful thoughts in the writing of this book.

My prayer is that the thoughts in this book may be helpful to the readers in their desire to grow spiritually and to believe they are very precious in God's sight.

Chapter One

But the fruit of the Spirit is LOVE, *joy, peace, patience, kindness, goodness, faithfulness, gentleness and self-control.*
—**Galatians 5:22–23**

I do not believe it is just a coincidence that the apostle Paul lists love first among the nine fruits of the Spirit. The entire story of the Bible centers around how much God loves us. There are numerous references in Scripture to God's love for His creation. Here are but a few:

> For God so loved the world that he gave his one and only Son, that whoever believes in him shall not perish but have eternal life.
>
> —**John 3:16**

> I have loved you with an everlasting love; I have drawn you with loving-kindness.
>
> —**Jeremiah 31:3**

> The LORD did not set his affection on you and choose you because you were more numerous than other peoples, for you

were the fewest of all peoples. But it was because the LORD loved you and kept the oath he swore to your forefathers . . .

—**Deuteronomy 7:7–8**

But God demonstrates his own love for us in this: While we were still sinners, Christ died for us.

—**Romans 5:8**

As the Father has loved me, so have I loved you. Now remain in my love.

—**John 15:9**

To allow God's love to grow within us becomes the fountain from which the other fruits of the Spirit issue forth. Love is a powerful description of God's relationship with us, His children. Those who have been loved as children by affectionate parents may find the concept of God's love easier to comprehend than those who have been reared primarily by command or punishment. To make the connection of understanding a loving God is much easier when parents have shown their children through actions and words how much they are loved.

What is a measurement of the fruit of love in its fullest? Perhaps the apostle Paul gives us the greatest inside view in his famous love chapter (1 Corinthians, chapter 13). First, Paul points out the supreme importance of having love above all other gifts:

If I speak in the tongues of men and of angels, but have not love, I am only a resounding gong or a clanging

2

cymbal. If I have the gift of prophecy and can fathom all mysteries and all knowledge, and if I have a faith that can move mountains, but have not love, I am nothing. If I give all I possess to the poor and surrender my body to the flames, but have not love, I gain nothing. (1–3)

Then he lists the characteristics of love:

Love is patient, love is kind. It does not envy, it does not boast, it is not proud. It is not rude, it is not self-seeking, it is not easily angered, it keeps no record of wrongs. Love does not delight in evil but rejoices with the truth. It always protects, always trusts, always hopes, always perseveres. (4–7)

Then Paul talks about the durability of this kind of love:

Love never fails. But where there are prophecies, they will cease; where there are tongues, they will be stilled; where there is knowledge, it will pass away. . . . And now these three remain: faith, hope, and love. But the greatest of these is love. (8, 13)

It could be said that faith has to do with the past. (I can have faith in you because of how I have observed you in past relationships.) Hope has to do with the future. (Because of my faith in you I can hope for the same of you in the future.) Love, however, has to do with today; the axis on which every experience in the present tense has significance.

We can have faith in God because of our awareness of His dependability in our past. We can hope that God's love

3

never changes and He will always be there! So, too, we can give ourselves to walking in His presence each day and letting His love more fully possess our inner soul.

Paul also writes about the gifts of the Holy Spirit, and in 1 Corinthians 12:28, he lists some:

> And in the church God has appointed first of all apostles, second prophets, third teachers, then workers of miracles, also those having gifts of healing, those able to help others, those with gifts of administration, and those speaking in different kinds of tongues.

However, there is a distinction to be made between gifts of the Spirit and fruits of the Spirit. For example, if I am talented with the gift of leadership and take advantage of the tools available to develop my capacity as a leader, that is one thing. But to develop a love for the people I work with and to develop patience, kindness, and so on—those come by my giving myself to the ways of the Holy Spirit. It doesn't necessarily follow that, by being a gifted leader, I automatically have the love for the people whom I lead. Fruits of the Spirit deal with the soul!

~

Cultivating Spiritual Fruit

Try writing letters to God (a powerful alternative method of praying), asking His Spirit to work within you in various ways so you can grow in love. Such letters might involve asking God:

- *to show you how you can grow in your own self-worth because He loves you so much*
- *for the ability to love your spouse in a way that perhaps has been difficult heretofore*
- *for wisdom and courage in parenting to help you convey love to your children as you set boundaries to help them to mature into responsible, trustworthy, and loving adults; celebrate their individual achievements; and set an example by your own actions*
- *for the capacity to resolve a resentment you may be harboring so you can forgive others*

These are just a few examples of how you can really grow in the capacity to love both yourself and others. It is vital you understand how precious you are to God; your cup of worth needs to run over unto others. You cannot give to others what you need for yourself. Remember, God loves you because you are you. He wants you to become all you can be through His love so you can truly be a blessing to both yourself and others.

Chapter Two

But the fruit of the Spirit is love, JOY, peace, patience, kindness,
goodness, faithfulness, gentleness and self-control.
—**Galatians 5:22–23**

Joy is often confused with happiness but the latter is only a byproduct of pleasurable feelings. Joy (as described by Paul) is much deeper. Let us consider just a few of the many biblical references to joy:

> Therefore, since we are surrounded by such a great cloud of witnesses, let us throw off everything that hinders and the sin that so easily entangles, and let us run with perseverance the race marked out for us. Let us fix our eyes on Jesus, the author and perfecter of our faith, who for the joy set before him endured the cross, scorning its shame, and sat down at the right hand of the throne of God.
>
> —**Hebrews 12:1–2**

> Consider it pure joy, my brothers, whenever you face trials of many kinds, because you know that the testing

of your faith develops perseverance. Perseverance must finish its work so that you may be mature and complete, not lacking anything.

—James 1:2–4

For to me, to live is Christ and to die is gain. If I am to go on living in the body, this will mean fruitful labor for me. Yet what shall I choose? I do not know! I am torn between the two: I desire to depart and be with Christ, which is better by far; but it is more necessary for you that I remain in the body. Convinced of this, I know that I will remain, and I will continue with all of you for your progress and joy in the faith, so that through my being with you again your joy in Christ Jesus will overflow on account of me.

—Philippians 1:21–26

As the Father has loved me, so have I loved you. Now remain in my love. If you obey my commands, you will remain in my love, just as I have obeyed my Father's commands and remain in his love. I have told you this so that my joy may be in you and that your joy may be complete.

—John 15:9–11

Let us also note a sampling of the many references in the book of Psalms about joy:

Surely you have granted him eternal blessings and made him glad with the joy of your presence.

—Psalm 21:6

Sing for joy to God our strength; shout aloud to
the God of Jacob!

—Psalm 81:1

You turned my wailing into dancing; you removed
my sackcloth and clothed me with joy, that my
heart may sing to you and not be silent. O LORD
my God, I will give you thanks forever.

—Psalm 30:11–12

Note that joy is inextricably related to our growing in the
awareness of God's love for us. It's like a state of being
wherein we can be in pain, undergo great obstacles, and carry
great burdens but still have this sense of joy because of a
commitment to do the best we know how as followers of
Jesus. This faithfulness to doing our best to be Christlike
gives us the assurance we will find the answers in all circumstances befalling us as we continue to keep in conversation
with God.

Now, consider the following passage:

One day Jesus was praying in a certain place. When
he finished, one of his disciples said to him, "Lord,
teach us to pray, just as John taught his disciples." He
said to them, "When you pray, say: 'Father, hallowed
be your name, your kingdom come. Give us each day
our daily bread. Forgive us our sins, for we also
forgive everyone who sins against us. And lead us not
into temptation.'"

—Luke 11:1–4

We call this the Lord's Prayer, a prayer Jesus taught His disciples and us to pray as a blueprint that leads to a joyful spirit. Consider four important points in this prayer:

1. **Scripture**: *Father, hallowed be your name, your kingdom come.*

   We are not praying for God to answer all our requests or fulfill all our needs as some sort of "waiter." We pray to discern what we truly know to be what God would want us to do; we ask to grow spiritually in discernment to understand His will for us.

2. **Scripture**: *Give us each day our daily bread.*

   This can be stated simply as "give us the ability to live one day at a time." Think of what we could be if we lived one day at a time rather than bringing all of yesterday's pain, junk, and mistakes into the todays and not spending the todays worrying about what is to come in the tomorrows!

3. **Scripture**: *Forgive us our sins, for we also forgive everyone who sins against us.*

   It is essential for our own spiritual well-being that we forgive and refuse to hold resentment.

4. **Scripture**: *And lead us not into temptation.*
   This has to do with our tomorrows—live each
   day fully and trust in God's guidance for our
   tomorrows.

Jesus tells this story immediately after His teaching about
prayer:

> Then he said to them, "Suppose one of you has a friend,
> and he goes to him at midnight and says, 'Friend, lend
> me three loaves of bread, because a friend of mine on a
> journey has come to me, and I have nothing to set before
> him.' Then the one inside answers, 'Don't bother me.
> The door is already locked, and my children are with me
> in bed. I can't get up and give you anything.' I tell you,
> though he will not get up and give him the bread because
> he is his friend, yet because of the man's boldness he will
> get up and give him as much as he needs."
>
> —Luke 11:5–8

What do you think Jesus is intimating here? I firmly believe
He wants us to struggle with God until we find an answer
that gives meaning to our soul, knowing that God is with us
always. I think we give up too easily and then arrive at the
conclusion that God doesn't care about us and doesn't seem
to give us answers.

My wonderful wife of more than fifty-seven years died
after several months of failing health, and I was angry with
God. Why, when I needed her more than ever, did she die?
For three months I harbored feelings of wanting to die and

11

be with her. I prayed morning and evening for God to answer my questions. I kept struggling with Him and raising the question, What now for me?

Then one morning a different outlook began to control my mind and soul. A peace began to fill me as I came to the realization that my wife was over her suffering and pain, and that God has her in His eternal care. I realized that God will always love me and we shall be together again some day.

Also, a new awareness began to fill my soul of the gifts I still have to share with others. I can live the remaining days of my life as a tribute to her and loving our children, grandchildren, and great-grandchildren.

Although I will always miss my wife, the emptiness has been gradually overshadowed by God's love which is greater than we can imagine. I have come to believe more firmly in God's love than ever before. I believe this is what joy is about—the conviction that God is with us always!

~

Cultivating Spiritual Fruit

Some ways we can grow in joy include:

- *reading Scripture and understanding the context in which passages are presented (For instance, Jesus speaks of joy on the evening of his arrest in Gethsemane, and Paul speaks of joy though he is in chains as a prisoner in Rome.)*
- *keeping a journal*

- *in difficult circumstances, ponder how God's presence can give you a sense of joy that you are never alone*

To try each day his will to know
To tread the way his will may show
To live for him who gave me life;
To strive for him who suffered strife
And sacrifice through death for me —
Let this my joy, my portion be.

—Author unknown

Chapter Three

But the fruit of the Spirit is love, joy, PEACE, patience, kindness, goodness, faithfulness, gentleness and self-control.
—Galatians 5:22–23

∼

Have you ever sat on the bank of a wide place in a flowing creek where the current seems not to move at all, and heard a few birds in the treetops overhead singing their solos? If so, perhaps you have experienced a feeling of peace and contentment and, for a time, the rest of the every day world seemed so far removed.

The word "peace" has many connotations, but most often, it's defined in what it is not. It's a term used in relation to warring nations, frequent acts of violence in any given community, family feuds, internal unrest because of what tomorrow may bring, as well as the hurts we cling to from the past and the guilt we seem to hang on to over the wrongs we have done to others. All such experiences we share in our world. How can we be at peace amidst all the things people do to one another, having to live with a disease slowly but surely eating away at our bodies, or even facing the many good-byes we must experience with significant people in our lives?

Peace is, however, one of the fruits of the Spirit. Let us consider a few biblical passages that give keener insight into what peace can mean:

> A heart at peace gives life to the body, but envy rots the bones.
>
> —**Proverbs 14:30**

> For to us a child is born, to us a son is given, and the government will be on his shoulders. And he will be called Wonderful Counselor, Mighty God, Everlasting Father, Prince of Peace.
>
> —**Isaiah 9:6**

> Peace I leave with you; my peace I give you. I do not give to you as the world gives. Do not let your hearts be troubled and do not be afraid.
>
> —**John 14:27**

> I have told you these things, so that in me you may have peace. In this world you will have trouble. But take heart! I have overcome the world.
>
> —**John 16:33**

> For he himself is our peace, who has made the two one and has destroyed the barrier, the dividing wall of hostility. . . .
>
> —**Ephesians 2:14**

And the peace of God, which transcends all understanding, will guard your hearts and your minds in
Christ Jesus.

—**Philippians 4:7**

Now may the Lord of peace himself give you peace at all
times and in every way. . . .

—**2 Thessalonians 3:16**

One of the world's great leaders, Mahatma Gandhi,
captured some of the essence of what these passages say
about peace when he stated: "Each one has to find his peace
from within. And peace to be real must be unaffected by
outside circumstances."

Years ago I experienced a situation never to be forgotten
in my pastoral ministry. One summer day I made a house
call on a young couple who had just become members of the
parish I served.

It was warm and the door was open. As I prepared to
knock on the screen door I heard a somewhat weak yell for
help, "Please come on in."

As I entered the family room I discovered an elderly
lady sitting in a rocking chair with a very small crying baby
now lying at her feet on the floor. She was the baby's great-
grandmother and had agreed to rock her to sleep while her
granddaughter made a quick trip to the pharmacy. The
baby had awakened, wrestled around in her arms, and
fallen out—the elderly woman had arthritis and couldn't
pick her up again. I picked up the baby and placed her in

her great-grandmother's arms, and the infant immediately quit crying and soon went sound to sleep.

I recall this story because the peace of which Paul writes is about our letting our souls be bathed by the ever-lasting love of the Heavenly Father. I believe the more personal our Lord Jesus becomes to us and the deeper our commitment we give to Him, the deeper the Holy Spirit gives us a sense of inner peace amidst all the other vicissitudes of the world in which we live. We can let ourselves be open to God's presence and experience this inner peace even though our bodies may be in pain, or we feel the anguish of life's stress—or even going through the sorrow and grief's work of letting a lifelong companion go to God's eternal care. There's no reason to despair when we get anxious as long as we have a deep yearning for this peace of which Paul writes and Jesus promised us.

～

Cultivating Spiritual Fruit

Commit yourself daily to reading all you can in the Bible about peace, praying each day for God's Spirit to have His way with you.

Focus daily on the presence of our Lord as your constant guide and friend, in addition to Him being your Savior.

Facing the cross in such a short time after His last supper with the disciples, Jesus told them, "My peace I give to you." Filled with a sense of God's unconditional love, we have an inner joy that bestows this sense of peace, knowing that in everything God has us in His care. Pray this prayer:

Father, take not away the burden of the day but help me bear it as Christ His burden bore when cross and thorn He wore and none with Him could share it; in His name, help, I pray! Amen.

Chapter Four

But the fruit of the Spirit is love, joy, peace, PATIENCE, kindness,
goodness, faithfulness, gentleness and self-control.
—**Galatians 5:22–23**

One spring a master gardener friend gave me a packet of tiny flower seeds, saying they made beautiful flowers but he didn't know what they were called. I planted them, carefully covered the two short rows with fine dirt, and kept them watered. It took ten days for tiny sprouts to appear. Patiently, I kept them moist and pulled the weeds away. In three months the bluish-green vines were almost two feet tall and covered with small, blue blossoms. The gift of patience finally bore fruit. Gardening can be good for the soul.

The apostle Paul delineates the results of a life without the Holy Spirit in Galatians 5:19–21, then goes on to contrast these acts with the gifts of the Spirit which come when we commit our lives to Jesus and experience the growth of our spiritual nature. Patience comes through keeping our soul in constant contact with the work of the Holy Spirit.

Consider the following biblical references to patience:

I waited patiently for the LORD; he turned to me and heard my cry.

—**Psalm 40:1**

A hot-tempered man stirs up dissension, but a patient man calms a quarrel.

—**Proverbs 15:18**

But if we hope for what we do not yet have, we wait for it patiently.

—**Romans 8:25**

In purity, understanding, patience and kindness; in the Holy Spirit and in sincere love . . .

—**2 Corinthians 6:6**

Be completely humble and gentle; be patient, bearing with one another in love.

—**Ephesians 4:2**

Being strengthened with all power according to his glorious might so that you may have great endurance and patience . . .

—**Colossians 1:11**

And we urge you, brothers, warn those who are idle, encourage the timid, help the weak, be patient with everyone.

—**1 Thessalonians 5:14**

One of the most beautiful stories of Jesus' patience, understanding, and healing is found in Matthew 15:21–28.

> Leaving that place, Jesus withdrew to the region of Tyre and Sidon. A Canaanite woman from that vicinity came to him, crying out, "Lord, Son of David, have mercy on me! My daughter is suffering terribly from demon-possession."
>
> Jesus did not answer a word. So his disciples came to him and urged him, "Send her away, for she keeps crying out after us."
>
> He answered, "I was sent only to the lost sheep of Israel."
>
> The woman came and knelt before him. "Lord, help me!" she said.
>
> He replied, "It is not right to take the children's bread and toss it to their dogs."
>
> "Yes, Lord," she said, "but even the dogs eat the crumbs that fall from their masters' table."
>
> Then Jesus answered, "Woman, you have great faith! Your request is granted." And her daughter was healed from that very hour.

Think about what is going on here between Jesus and His disciples, the disciples and this woman, and this woman and Jesus. Jesus and the disciples are on a retreat when a Canaanite woman approaches Jesus, and with a desperate mother's heart due to her daughter's illness, begs for her daughter's healing.

Jesus remains silent, and why do the disciples want to send her away? Is it because she is not of Jewish background, because they want to protect Jesus, or both?

The mother pays no attention to the disciples; her eyes are fixed on Jesus. They are having a wordless conversation, patiently understanding each other's position.

Finally, Jesus says, "I was sent only to the lost sheep of Israel," to which the woman pays no attention, because she is in tune with His healing love for all who come for help.

Then He says to her (which many may think was absolute cruelty), "It is not right to take the children's bread and toss it to the dogs." (A slang expression among some Jews was that outsiders were considered only as dogs.)

The woman, however, picked up on His patient humor immediately with the words, "Yes, Lord, but even the dogs eat the crumbs that fall from their masters' table." What persistence this woman manifested! What perseverance and endurance she would undergo for her daughter! What faith she had in this one called Jesus!

So, we get an inside picture of the tremendous faith this mother had in Jesus. She would not take no for an answer, but more than that, she knew His heart. We also see the patience of the Master to keep the dialogue of the heart continuing so that she—and we—can receive the blessings He bestows.

May our desire for that inner patience cause us to persevere with our devotion to God's presence and allow the Spirit to deepen our sense of spiritual victory!

~

Cultivating Spiritual Fruit

Practice the presence of Jesus. Begin by breathing deeply, filling your lungs to capacity. Hold your breath for two seconds, slowly exhale, and silently say the words: "The Lord is my shepherd, I shall not want."

Close your eyes, continue exhaling and inhaling, and continue saying the words: "The Lord is my shepherd, I shall not want." Visualize all the stress, tension, and anxiousness leaving your body, beginning with the scalp of your head and eventually flowing out the toes of both feet.

Proceed slowly with the inhalations and exhalations, repeating over and over again: "The Lord is my shepherd, I shall not want" until you have visualized your entire body being relieved of all stress, anxious feelings, and tension.

Practice this exercise for two weeks, each evening as you retire for sleep and each morning as you prepare to rise for the day.

May the God of all comfort grant you the patience to persevere!

Chapter Five

But the fruit of the Spirit is love, joy, peace, patience, KINDNESS, goodness, faithfulness, gentleness and self-control.
—**Galatians 5:22–23**

Of the nine fruits of the Spirit listed by Paul, perhaps kindness seems the more noticeable to other people. Love could be thought of as the cradle from which all the other fruits develop; that is, the more we let God's unconditional love saturate our inner being, the better chances we will have of growing into these other characteristics. But kindness is manifested in how we talk to people, in the ability to read the soul of another person, and in speaking words that move the heart, and not just intellectual words.

When my wife died, a clinical psychologist with whom I worked came to me and said, "You have given so much to others as chaplain and I want you to know that myself and others here in the hospital want to help you through your sorrow with whatever we can to let you know we all care." Those are words of kindness!

Kindness is not to be mistaken for self-abasement, timidity, cowardice, a surrendering of one's identity to live up to another's expectations, or the like. Kindness is just the opposite—the opposite of our self-worthfulness in such a way that our cup just naturally runs over in the touching of others, regardless of how we feel about them.

Kindness is powerful. It can make an enemy into a friend and can lift up another who is at wit's end in grief, pain, and emotional confusion. Kindness speaks of helping another person down on his or her economic means, perhaps of helping with children or sharing financially if at all possible, and of listening to another person who just needs to vent.

Look at what Proverbs 25:21–22 says about kindness:

> If your enemy is hungry, give him food to eat; if he is thirsty, give him water to drink. In doing this, you will heap burning coals on his head, and the Lord will reward you.

Paul also quotes this passage in Romans 12:20. However, I do not think an act of kindness ought to be given to make another feel guilty or shameful because of their ill intentions towards us. Kindness issues from an overflowing heart of love. If it does, however, provoke a sense of creative shame or guilt to the receiver that changes his or her perspective on life—wonderful!

A while back, I was in a department store and made a purchase. The saleswoman never smiled, nor did she say a word. She wrote up the sale, opened the cash register, took the receipt, put the item in a sack, and handed it to me.

I said to her, "Thank you so much. I cannot help but believe you are having a bad day."

To which the tears began to flow. "Yes, I am," she replied. "My husband, after being married fourteen years, said yesterday he wanted a divorce."

I urged her to remember that her life is too important to allow anything to bring her down and suggested she seek some mutual help. The no-longer silent woman thanked me profusely and said my words helped restore her faith in people.

Following are some biblical passages which speak of kindness:

> An anxious heart weighs a man down, but a kind word cheers him up.
> —Proverbs 12:25

> He who despises his neighbor sins, but blessed is he who is kind to the needy.
> —Proverbs 14:21

> He who is kind to the poor lends to the LORD, and he will reward him for what he has done.
> —Proverbs 19:17

> Consider therefore the kindness and sternness of God: sternness to those who fell, but kindness to you, provided that you continue in his kindness.
> —Romans 11:22

> Love is patient, love is kind. It does not envy, it does not boast, it is not proud.
> —1 Corinthians 13:4

Get rid of all bitterness, rage and anger, brawling and slander, along with every form of malice. Be kind and compassionate to one another, forgiving each other, just as in Christ God forgave you.

—Ephesians 4:31–32

For this very reason, make every effort to add to your faith goodness; and to goodness, knowledge; and to knowledge, self-control; and to self-control, perseverance; and to perseverance, godliness; and to godliness, brotherly kindness; and to brotherly kindness, love.

—2 Peter 1:5–7

One of the many stories reflecting the great kindness of our Lord is recorded in Mark 10:13–16.

People were bringing little children to Jesus to have him touch them, but the disciples rebuked them. When Jesus saw this, he was indignant. He said to them, "Let the little children come to me, and do not hinder them, for the kingdom of God belongs to such as these. I tell you the truth, anyone who will not receive the kingdom of God like a little child will never enter it." And he took the children in his arms, put his hands on them and blessed them.

One must understand the situation in which this story unfolds. Crowds of people were following Jesus as He was at the height of His popularity. At one point Jesus was addressed by some of the religious leaders of Israel on a subject and He began talking to them. A crowd gathered that included mothers wanting their little children to see this man who performed miracles, taught with such authority, and seemed so kind. In that culture, there was also the belief that if a child could touch the hem of an outer garment of a religious leader, it would bless the child. So, the mothers allowed the children to weave their way though the crowd to be able to see Jesus and have Him bless them.

The disciples were indignant and called out to the mothers, "Don't you see the Master is too busy to be disturbed by your children?" or some such words. One can picture the shame some of the mothers had at such a rebuke.

But the kind Savior saw an opportunity to teach one of the most vital insights about our becoming a part of the kingdom of God. He called for the children to gather round Him. He gathered them one by one in His arms, blessed them, and said, "of such is the kingdom of heaven."

What did He mean by such words? Children are trusting, honest, and genuine. Children are loving and respond to loving actions and words—and those are just some of the attributes of a small child!

Adults can become so hard because of the knocks life often gives us and the difficult times we endure that we often fail to grasp the meaning of trusting in God and believing in His promises.

Kindness can:

- *change our entire perspective on life—whether we offer kindness to someone or are on the receiving end*

- *erase bitterness (If you have resentment against someone, pray to God constantly to have this resentment removed and see how different your life can be.)*

- *open the door for others to have a new outlook on life; by such you become God's hands to bless people*

- *light a candle for both yourself and others when darkness descends and seems to overshadow hope*

- *expand the joy of living because it gives a sense of purpose and direction to your life instead of wanting to give up*

- *do more for the giver than the receiver, and give contentment*

Kindness costs nothing except having to give up any self-centeredness, pride, resentment, or desire for revenge, or any sense of callousness for having to undergo any hard knocks which may come our way. Kindness feeds the embers of the soul as to how much we are really loved of God, the Father!

God wants you to be kind for your sake as well as in ministering on His behalf to others!

~

Cultivating Spiritual Fruit

Make a list of some unhealthy attitudes you may have about life and about others. Make a list of small kindnesses you can begin making and practice just one each day—one step at a time—knowing God is with you every step of the way!

Chapter Six

But the fruit of the Spirit is love, joy, peace, patience, kindness,
GOODNESS, *faithfulness, gentleness and self-control.*

—Galatians 5:22–23

When I think of goodness, the person of Barnabas comes to mind. Though there are few references to him, each one highlighted his tremendous importance in the early days of Christianity. Barnabas is the person of whom Luke writes: "He was a good man, full of the Holy Spirit and faith. . . ." (Acts 11:24). Five very important aspects of this "good" man are listed in Acts.

1. He sold a field and gave all the proceeds to the apostles to distribute to those in need in the early Christian community (4:36–37).

2. He interceded on behalf of Paul (then known as Saul), who went to the church at Jerusalem after his conversion on the road to Damascus. The

church was fearful of Paul because of his past persecution of Christians (9:26–27).

3. When a large group of people in Antioch believed, the church at Jerusalem sent Barnabas there to work with them. Barnabas went to Tarsus and got Paul (then Saul), opening the door for Paul to begin his tremendous work for which Jesus had personally called him (11:25–26).

4. Barnabas was the leader of the early Christian movement in Tarsus, yet we note the great humility of Barnabas in the first missionary journey as Paul soon seemed to be at the fore-front (13:1–13). Note that up to this point it was Barnabas and Saul (later known as Paul). From 13:13 on, it was always Paul and Barnabas.

5. Barnabas's cousin, John Mark, returned to Jerusalem during the first missionary journey, so Paul refused to take him along on the second. Barnabas, however, saw the great potential in this young man, so he and John Mark set out separate from Paul (15:36–39).

Note just a few of the multiple references to goodness in the Bible:

Taste and see that the LORD is good; blessed is the man who takes refuge in him.

—Psalm 34:8

Trust in the LORD and do good . . .

—Psalm 37:3

A cheerful heart is good medicine, but a crushed spirit dries up the bones.

—Proverbs 17:22

A good name is more desirable than great riches; to be esteemed is better than silver or gold.

—Proverbs 22:1

He has showed you, O man, what is good. And what does the LORD require of you? To act justly and to love mercy and to walk humbly with your God.

—Micah 6:8

The good man brings good things out of the good stored up in him, and the evil man brings evil things out of the evil stored up in him.

—Matthew 12:35

I am the good shepherd.

—John 10:11

Goodness is at the very heart of a godly person's character; it cannot be feigned. One may seemingly act kind towards another, or one may feign patience and gentleness, but goodness would be hard to fake since several of the other fruits naturally issue forth from goodness. To do good for "goodness's sake" is not for praise or reward. Yet the rewards of goodness can be great. With goodness, one receives inner peace, lack of a sense of guilt or shame, and consequently, shares in the very nature of God.

Goodness can grow within the human spirit because God is not finished with us in this life. Consider Philippians 1:3–6, which reads:

> I thank my God every time I remember you. In all my prayers for all of you, I always pray with joy because of your partnership in the gospel from the first day until now, being confident of this, that he who began a good work in you will carry it on to completion until the day of Christ Jesus.

This is one of the joys you and I can always treasure: we can continue to grow into Christlikeness and not be discouraged when our behavior doesn't always live up to our intentions. We need to assure ourselves that God is right there beside us and within us to help us bring the buds of goodness to flower. You and I will not be perfect in this life but that is not the point, it is to feel God has a purpose for us and that He will continue to work His righteousness within us as we continue to focus on His goodness and mercy. We are God's works in progress. Paul wrote the following to the Corinthian church:

Now the Lord is the Spirit, and where the Spirit of the Lord is, there is freedom. And we, who with unveiled faces all reflect the Lord's glory, are being transformed into his likeness with ever-increasing glory, which comes from the Lord, who is the Spirit.

—2 Corinthians 3:17–18

We don't just declare that we are going to be good, nor is it to be bought. Like the other fruits of the Spirit, goodness is the work of the Lord upon us. We let our souls be open to God's presence and His Spirit silently but surely is at work, making all things new from day to day within us. When we allow all the windows of our soul to be open to Him, He does the transformation from one degree of glory to another. That is the mystery of the grace of God: He works His wonders within us when we make ourselves available to Him. It is a mystery how God impregnates a piece of rock with gems of gold, and how He forms a beautiful diamond. You are precious in His sight! Do the best you can—dare to allow a spirit of goodness to gradually take hold in your life!

When President Harry Truman's term in office ended, I was only a young man. I became an ardent admirer of him because of his character. Truman didn't have a college degree but possessed a quality of character that caused many of his critics to change their evaluation of him upon personal interaction with him.

David McCullough, in his book, *Truman*, tells the story of novelist Merle Miller who was assigned to collaborate

37

with Truman on some of his memoirs. Miller had a cynical view towards the president before meeting him, but after several face-to-face conversations with him, Miller later wrote about Truman:

> If I had a father who was smart, or if I had a father who read a book, if I had a father who knew how to get along with people . . . this was he [Truman] . . . How could you not like him! He was such a decent human being with concern, a genuine concern for your welfare.
>
> "Well, how are you?" "How's your hotel?" "How's the food?" . . . He wanted to make you comfortable, and he did make you comfortable. I never had an uncomfortable moment with him except toward the end when it appeared there was never going to be a show . . . You could reach out to him and there was somebody there. There was a person there! . . . HE WAS THERE FOR YOU.[1]

Goodness has so many facets but in its presence one always feels cared for, understood, helped, and motivated to be a better person for having been in its presence.

~

Cultivating Spiritual Fruit

Please take a trip back through your childhood years and up to your present age. Write the names of as many people as you can remember whose goodness of character made an impact on you (parent, grandparent, teacher, minister, etc.) to be the very best person you could be and in what ways they helped shape your own life for the good.

Along with these memories, now focus on the areas of your life in which you can be further blessed as you focus on God's unconditional love for you. Reach out to someone close to you that they may experience the goodness of your person on their lives.

May God bless you as you continue praying for God's guidance and His love to overshadow you each day to come!

Chapter Seven

But the fruit of the Spirit is love, joy, peace, patience, kindness, goodness, FAITHFULNESS, *gentleness and self-control.*

—**Galatians 5:22–23**

Continuing to be faithful to commitments we have made sometimes becomes difficult, especially when we become discouraged or lose heart. Years ago in high school I decided to try out for track events because I believed I was a good runner. I set my goal as a freshman to be the best mile runner in the school.

In my freshman year, the coach didn't think I was cut out for distance; he felt I was good at short distances where speed was most important. However, in my sophomore year he felt I had great potential because I kept running every day.

It was not until my junior year that I began to excel because I had learned five very important disciplines to be a distance runner: (1) how to avoid speeding ahead the first quarter-mile so my legs wouldn't give out; (2) how to pace my running, moving my feet much differently and taking longer strides, and how to pace my breathing so as not to become short-winded; (3) how to avoid "hitting the wall" (an expression meaning running out of energy most distance runners know all too well); (4) how to gauge my breathing in that all-important third quarter-mile; and, finally, (5) how to have the will to give it all I had, though tired, the last half of the fourth quarter-mile. I did, in fact, become the best mile runner in the school during my senior year.

Paul writes about being faithful to our commitment to let Christ become the centerpiece of our lives, growing in our steadfastness to the best we know of His will for our lives, when seemingly, so many circumstances would almost make this impossible.

In Hebrews 12:1–3 we read of a great arena filled with a great audience of those who have gone before us as we run the race of a devoted life:

> Therefore, since we are surrounded by such a great cloud of witnesses, let us throw off everything that hinders and the sin that so easily entangles, and let us run with perseverance the race marked out for us. Let us fix our eyes on Jesus, the author and perfecter of our faith, who for the joy set before him endured the cross, scorning its shame, and sat down at the right hand of the throne of God. Consider him who endured such opposition from sinful men, so that you will not grow weary and lose heart.

Consider the twelve disciples who traveled with Jesus for three years. They were all scattered during His trial. They fled when the going got tough. In the upper room, Jesus told them He was leaving and said they would not be able to go with Him (John 13:33).

Peter asked Him, "Lord, where are you going?" and then declared the following, "Lord, why can't I follow you now? I will lay down my life for you" (John 13:36–37).

Jesus then replied, "Will you really lay down your life for me? I tell you the truth, before the rooster crows, you will disown me three times!" (John 13:38).

Remember how remorseful Peter became because of his shallowness of commitment when the going got tough? Also note how Peter's lack of commitment became the seedbed for an unwavering commitment to follow Jesus after His resurrection—a commitment that caused Peter to eventually be crucified. He even asked to be crucified upside down, thinking it unworthy to be crucified in the same manner as his Lord. What commitment that turned out to be!

Faithfulness to make Christ the centerpiece of our lives and to focus on His love for us helps prepare our souls for the Spirit to recreate a new being inside us. This helps feed faithfulness to all the worthwhile ventures we embark on to be useful servants of Him during our lifetime.

Here, let us consider some helpful biblical passages dealing with faithfulness:

> For the word of the LORD is right and true; he is faithful in all he does.
>
> —Psalm 33:4

Your kingdom is an everlasting kingdom, and your dominion endures through all generations. The LORD is faithful to all his promises and loving toward all he has made.

—Psalm 145:13

[The LORD is] the Maker of heaven and earth, the sea, and everything in them—the LORD, who remains faithful forever.

—Psalm 146:6

Be joyful in hope, patient in affliction, faithful in prayer.
—Romans 12:12

Here is a trustworthy saying: If we died with him, we will also live with him; if we endure, we will also reign with him. If we disown him, he will also disown us; if we are faithless, he will remain faithful, for he cannot disown himself.

—2 Timothy 2:11–13

Be faithful, even to the point of death, and I will give you the crown of life.

—Revelation 2:10

The story of Job perhaps represents the best the Old Testament has of making sense of God's purposes for our lives even though at times we ask why. In Job 13:15 is the declaration of Job in response to all the sufferings, tragedies, and diseases that plagued his life: "Though he slay me, yet will I hope in him."

Some questions we ask cannot be answered in this life, yet we still sometimes ask why. Why do the seemingly righteous suffer? Why does a companion with whom we lived most of our adult lives die when we have come to love them so much? Why does hate seem to triumph over love at times? Why? We need to keep struggling with God until we find answers that enable us to keep on trusting because if we do not have God, we have nothing to hold on to at all! We must remain faithful in our belief that God will give us meaning and victory, if not in this life, then in the life to come, because our eternity with God is not measured in terms of years in this earthly life; we have been created for eternity in God!

As we remain faithful to God, we will find it easier to be faithful in our many commitments in life:

- **Faithfulness to our partner in our wedding vows**

  Infidelity does more harm to us than to our spouse because we have been unfaithful to the highest we know within our very souls; and yet, God can create a new sense of commitment as we turn to Him, accept forgiveness, and go on to a higher sense of love one for another.

- **Faithfulness as parents**

  There may never be perfect parents but parenting is being faithful to the best we know of loving our children and setting the examples for them in our own living and relationships to them.

- **Faithfulness in our job commitments and in doing the best we can**

- **Faithfulness as a friend when friends struggle**
  We can be there to help the best we know how.
- **Faithfulness as adult children to our parents**
  We forgive them for the mistakes they might have made because forgiveness is so necessary for the well being of our own souls.
- **Faithfulness in our word to others**
  Let our words be as honor-bound as any written contract we may have.

Above all, we must be faithful to the best within ourselves. If we fall short, continue practicing the presence of God until we receive inner renewal and go on to higher things through God's unconditional love for us. That is why love is the first fruit of the Spirit. Paul lists a love for the worthfulness of our own selves because God created us and God doesn't make junk, but rather works in continuous progress until the day of perfection when we enter the eternal glory with Him.

~

Cultivating Spiritual Fruit

This is a spiritual exercise to help strengthen your desire to follow through for some noble goal, to overcome some weakness of character, or to reach out and follow through on promises you have made when the going seems tough.

Please read Hebrews 12:1–3 again. The writer is depicting an arena in which spectators in the bleachers are rooting for you on the playing field of life. These spectators may be significant people in your life who have died and, from heaven, are all supporting you, along with the blessed Lord who leads the cheering section.

Focus on how you can gain renewed strength to remain faithful in the achievement of that significant goal, to follow through to overcome some weakness of character, or to follow through with promises you have made to significant others when temptations call you aside. Feel the Holy Spirit pulsing through your spiritual veins, giving you new strength and perseverance. I suggest you use this exercise often, until it becomes as regular as any physical exercise you may do for bodily health. Remember, Jesus said, "I am with you always, to the very end of the age" (Matt. 28:20).

Chapter Eight

But the fruit of the Spirit is love, joy, peace, patience, kindness, goodness, faithfulness, GENTLENESS *and self-control.*
—Galatians 5:22–23

~

The most graphic example of gentleness that comes to my mind is the entire saga of how God came to earth through His Son and the events that brought forth the most triumphant victory over evil. Think of the birth of Jesus. He was born in a manger, a stable, because there was no room in the inn. Not an appropriate entrance into the world for a powerful potentate.

The most paradoxical scene of all, however, is what we call the "triumphal entry," recorded in all four of the gospels.

Matthew, writing his gospel primarily to a Jewish audience, quotes more from the Old Testament than the others. Jesus directed two of His disciples to go the village ahead and ask for a particular donkey:

This took place to fulfill what was spoken through the prophet: "Say to the Daughter of Zion, 'See, your king comes to you, gentle and riding on a donkey, on a colt, the foal of a donkey.'"

—Matthew 21:4–5

Being the son of a farmer, growing up on the farm, and working with horses, I remember a special yoke used to break in a new horse. The horse didn't have to pull its full share, just learn to keep up with the veteran horse and develop the discipline of togetherness. Such a yoke broke with gentleness. I always think of it when I think of Christ riding that as-yet unbroken donkey.

Jesus brings forgiveness and new life to those who surrender their lives to His gentle, but powerful, might over sin and hell.

Do you recall the words of the story "One Solitary Life," credited by some as being from a sermon by Dr. James Allan Francis (1864–1928)?

He was born in an obscure village,
the child of a peasant woman.
He grew up in still another obscure village where he worked
in a carpenter shop until he was thirty . . .
He did none of the things one usually
associates with greatness.
He had no credentials but himself.
He was only thirty-three when the tide of popular opinion
turned against him . . .

He was turned over to his enemies . . .
and was nailed upon a cross
When he was dead he was laid in a borrowed grave . . .
Nineteen centuries have come and gone and TODAY
he is the central figure of the human race . . .
No one has affected the life of mankind on earth
as much as that ONE SOLITARY LIFE!

The apostle Paul was undoubtedly the greatest evangelist in all the history of Christendom. He pastored the churches that began with his preaching; as a pastor, he always strove for spiritual growth. We can grow from one degree of glory to another as we allow our souls to be in constant communion with the Holy Spirit. Paul lists gentleness among the nine fruits of the Spirit. Other biblical passages lifting up the worth of a gentle spirit include:

A gentle answer turns away wrath, but a harsh word stirs up anger.

—**Proverbs 15:1**

Let your gentleness be evident to all.

—**Philippians 4:5**

By the meekness and gentleness of Christ, I appeal to you . . .

—**2 Corinthians 10:1**

But you, man of God, flee from all this, and pursue righteousness, godliness, faith, love, endurance and gentleness.
—1 Timothy 6:11

But in your hearts . . . be prepared to give an answer to
everyone who asks you to give the reason for the hope that
you have. But do this with gentleness and respect. . . .
—1 Peter 3:15

Gentleness has not any of the loud noise of a clap of
thunder, yet it has the power of a lightning bolt to change
things. Gentleness is being considerate and humble, and
emanates from a soul that has its own security. Gentleness has
an air of authenticity about it that others notice. This fruit of
the Spirit becomes part of the glue that holds family relationships together among other of the fruits of the Spirit. A gentle
spirit knows the power of two of the shortest sentences in relationships, the ability to say I love you and I am sorry.

❧

Cultivating Spiritual Fruit

When under great stress over a situation that blows your
cool, project yourself ten years down the way and then reflect
back upon this seemingly great stress. How important was it
really? As I look back across the years of my life, many
stressful and seemingly world-shaking events I faced weren't
worth the paper to write them down.

Here's another suggestion: Picture one of the gentlest
persons you know, then write a letter to that person—but do

not mail it. Write what traits of gentleness this person exemplifies and try practicing them with others. Turn the letter over to God in your prayer, that He might help you to grow in this kind of gentleness.

One of the most helpful exercises I have found is to place a chair in front of me and imagine Jesus sitting there. I pour out my soul to Him and talk about my faults and ask how I can grow to be more gentle, kind, loving, and understanding. Then I listen to what Jesus would tell me. I try to picture His presence with me at all times.

God bless you and be with you as you desire to grow in His gentle ways!

Chapter Nine

But the fruit of the Spirit is love, joy, peace, patience,
kindness, goodness, faithfulness, gentleness and SELF-CONTROL.
Against such things there is no law.
—**Galatians 5:22–23**

As humans, we must live in community, and there is a fine line between being ourselves and asserting our individuality and what makes a community, working together for the mutual good of each person. One can read the laws of community councils, state legislatures, and governments to understand the transgressions individuals commit in doing what they want to do at the expense of others' rights and privileges.

Paul lists self-control as the last of the nine. That could be because our growing in the other eight fruits of the Spirit produces self-control as a natural byproduct. The more we grow in love, joy, peace, and all the other fruits, it is much easier to control our passions, self-indulgence, and self-seeking ways. One who cannot control his or her own passions will be unable to influence others for wholesome-ness of living and unable to effectively lead others. As we continue to grow in God's love and experience the joy of believing in His constant care, we can better understand what is right in itself, good and proper, in following the inner Spirit's leadings!

It is not by chance that young human beings are dependent on the nurture and discipline of parents or other authority figures. Well-rounded parenting nurtures children in the ways of love and gentleness, while providing discipline in order to develop an effective conscience as they mature into adulthood. We guide children through our own examples of maturity so as not to give in to self-serving attitudes.

There is no law imputing any of the fruits of the Spirit, however, except the unbridled passions Paul writes about in Galatians 5:19–21. Even in the natural law, children can grow to believe certain principles are inherently right and learn that seeking the good of others is the best way of interpersonal well-being. Individuals can mature in such a way as to seek their inner guidance to determine what values they must live by and how they must treat others and themselves to have self-respect and the respect of the community.

To be able to grow in our ability to self-regulate is absolutely necessary to live at peace in our world and at peace within ourselves.

Following are some of the biblical passages that accentuate the worthfulness of self-control:

> Like a city whose walls are broken down is a man who lacks self-control.
>
> —**Proverbs 25:28**

56

Now the overseer must be above reproach, the husband of but one wife, temperate, self-controlled, respectable, hospitable, able to teach, not given to drunkenness, not violent but gentle, not quarrelsome, not a lover of money.

—1 Timothy 3:2–3

Teach the older men to be temperate, worthy of respect, self-controlled, and sound in faith, in love and in endurance.

—Titus 2:2

Similarly, encourage the young men to be self-controlled.

—Titus 2:6

For the grace of God that brings salvation has appeared to all men. It teaches us to say "No" to ungodliness and worldly passions, and to live self-controlled, upright and godly lives in this present age . . .

—Titus 2:11–12

Therefore, prepare your minds for action; be self-controlled; set your hope fully on the grace to be given you when Jesus Christ is revealed.

—1 Peter 1:13

Attempting to grow in self-control undoubtedly will have its setbacks. Remember, though: You are not perfect; you are a work in progress as you continue to give your soul for the leading of the Spirit. You are being reborn every day, so when mistakes come, you can allow them to become the fertile ground for a better harvest; in day-by-day living you can let the God-image within you take better control of your spirit, through creative guilt and a greater dependence on the leading of the Holy Spirit.

~

Cultivating Spiritual Fruit

1. Set goals each week in reaching out to others in a way that might make you vulnerable, for it is in our vulnerability that we grow the spiritual muscles to become stronger in our own self-control.

2. Risk new paths of self-discipline. Remember, what we eat, what we may be free to do, and what we will do if Spirit-driven makes the difference!

3. Risk doing without instead of going further into debt.

4. Risk giving to others more of that which you do not need beyond the necessities. You will have a deeper inner peace for having done so.

Add to this list other exercises you can try to allow the peace of a self-controlled life to grow even more.

Greatness

What makes a man great? Is it houses and lands?
Is it argosies dropping their wealth at his feet?
Is it multitudes shouting his name in the street?
Is it power of brain? Is it skill of hand?
Is it writing a book? Is it guiding the State?
Nay, nay, none of these can make a man great.

The crystal burns cold with its beautiful fire,
And is what it is; it can never be more;
The acorn, with something wrapped warm at the core,
In quietness says, "To the oak I aspire."
That something in seed and in tree is the same —
What makes a man great is his greatness of aim.

What is greatness of aim? Your purpose to trim
For bringing the world to obey your behest?
O no, it is seeking God's perfect and best,
Making something the same both in you and in him.
Love what he loves, and, child of the sod,
Already you share in the greatness of God.

—Samuel V. Cole[1]

59

Epilogue

It is my fervent prayer that you who read this book will be as blessed and motivated to want to continue growing spiritually as I have been blessed in putting my thoughts on paper. I pray that I will continue to grow spiritually as long as God gives me life on this earth, and that I may be a help to others in their spiritual journey as well as receive spiritual strength from them.

I have learned through the years that sometimes what can be counted doesn't really count, and that what counts in life can't always be counted! Success in this life depends on who we really become as God's children, in making this world a better place in which to live, and in our becoming windows through which God's wonderful love shines in blessing another human being!

> God is love. Whoever lives in love lives in God, and God in him. In this way, love is made complete among us so that we will have confidence on the day of judgment, because in this world we are like him. There is no fear in love. But perfect love drives out fear, because fear has to do with punishment. The one who fears is not made perfect in love. We love because he first loved us.
>
> —1 John 4:16–19

Notes

Chapter 6

1. David McCullough, *Truman* (New York: Simon and Schuster, 1992), 997.

Chapter 9

1. James Mudge, ed., *Poems with Power to Strengthen the Soul* (Nashville, Tenn: Abingdon Cokesbury Press, 1935), 284.

THE
AUTHOR

Paul L. Kitley

A native of Shelby County, Indiana, Paul L. Kitley has made it his life's work to serve God's people through church ministry and counseling. He received a bachelor of arts degree from Butler University before earning his master of divinity and doctor of ministry degrees from Indianapolis's Christian Theological Seminary. He also completed post-doctorate studies in counseling theory and practice.

Kitley was ordained into the ministry of the Christian Church (Disciples of Christ) in 1949, and spent twenty-nine years in parish ministry. From 1981 to 1994, he served as director of the Lafayette Pastoral Counseling Center, where he practiced individual, family, and marital therapy; he has also conducted seminars throughout the Indiana region and local community.

A licensed marriage and family therapist and licensed clinical social worker, Kitley is a fellow in the American Association of Pastoral Counselors and a clinical member of the American Association for Marital and Family Therapy.

Kitley has served as dean of the College of Fellows in the international Academy of Parish Clergy. He has taught seminars in marriage enrichment, family communications, personal growth, and conflict management.

Kitley and his wife, Justine, were married for almost fifty-eight years before her death in 2005. They have three children and seven grandchildren. Kitley lives in Lafayette, Indiana, where he maintains a limited practice in pastoral psychotherapy.